NORTHAMPTONSHIRE

GHOST STORIES

Compiled by Julia Skinner

THE FRANCIS FRITH COLLECTION

www.francisfrith.com

First published in the United Kingdom in 2011 by The Francis Frith Collection®

This edition published exclusively for Identity Books in 2011 ISBN 978-1-84589-569-3

British Library Cataloguing in Publication Data

Haunted Northamptonshire - Ghost Stories
Compiled by Julia Skinner

The Francis Frith Collection
Oakley Business Park, Wylye Road,
Dinton, Wiltshire SP3 5EU
Tel: +44 (0) 1722 716 376
Email: info@francisfrith.co.uk
www.francisfrith.com

Printed and bound in Malaysia

Front Cover: **KETTERING, THE MARKET 1922** 72232p
Frontispiece: **NORTHAMPTON, ABINGTON STREET 1922** 72171

The colour-tinting is for illustrative purposes only, and is not intended to be historically accurate

AS WITH ANY HISTORICAL DATABASE, THE FRANCIS FRITH ARCHIVE IS CONSTANTLY BEING CORRECTED AND IMPROVED, AND THE PUBLISHERS WOULD WELCOME INFORMATION ON OMISSIONS OR INACCURACIES

CONTENTS

2 Haunted Northamptonshire

54 Francis Frith - Pioneer Victorian Photographer

NORTHAMPTON, FROM ALL SAINTS TOWER 1922 72166

DORMAN
DORMAN

HAUNTED NORTHAMPTONSHIRE

Northampton, the county town of Northamptonshire, has a long history. In the Anglo-Saxon period Northampton prospered as a river port and trading centre – its situation, where the River Nene cuts through the limestone ridge, provided an ideal defensive position, as well as the control over a river crossing where key routes converged. After the Norman Conquest of 1066 the strategic value of the town was recognised by the building of a castle, which was used as an occasional royal residence during the Middle Ages. Northampton Castle is now no longer to be seen, for it suffered not one but two cruel fates: the first was in 1662, after King Charles II was restored to the throne after the Civil War of the 17th century, when the king took vengeance on the pro-Parliamentarian town of Northampton by ordering its castle to be slighted, so that it would not be of any future military use to rebels against the throne. A fair amount of the castle survived this treatment, only to succumb in the 19th century when the railway station was built across its site in 1879.

Northampton witnessed many important events during the Middle Ages. The town held both the forerunner of parliament (in the form of a great royal council) and full parliaments, before these finally settled in the royal palace of Westminster after following the king around the country. The royal council first met in Northampton from King Stephen's reign (1135-54). The first parliament attended by burgesses or merchants, the forerunners of the members of the House of Commons, was held at Northampton in 1179. After the Barons' Wars of the 1260s, when Northampton was besieged and captured from Simon de Montfort, the rebellious barons' leader, several parliaments were held here, including the notorious one of 1380 when the first poll tax was passed. This unpopular measure provoked the Peasants' Revolt of the following year. Medieval Northampton stretched eastwards from the river and castle, with Market Square as its focus. The medieval town walls enclosed about

245 acres, with St Giles Church near the east gate and the Church of the Holy Sepulchre towards the north gate. The town walls were demolished at the same time as the castle was 'slighted' by order of Charles II in 1662.

For many centuries Northampton was famous for its important boot- and shoe-making industry: it is known that over 4,000 pairs of leather shoes and 600 pairs of cavalry jack-boots were made here for the Parliamentary armies during the Civil War of the 17th century. By the early 18th century Northampton had long been a noted supplier of footwear to the army, as well as to civilians and the American colonies. 'Brabner's Gazetteer of England and Wales' listed the industries of Northampton in 1895, showing that boot- and shoe-making and the associated trades were still one of the mainstays of Northampton's economy: 'Immense quantities of boots and shoes are still made for the supply of the army, the London market and for exportation. A large trade is also carried on in the tanning and currying of leather.'

Northampton suffered a devastating town fire in 1675. The Great Fire started in a thatched cottage in St Mary's Street and quickly spread eastwards, fanned by a strong wind which was aptly described by the Town Clerk of the time as 'The wind was very strong to blow ye fire on, but it was God who blew ye bellows'. The fire consumed three-quarters of the town (estimated at 600 houses), including Horse Fair, Market Square and Abington Street. Very little survived the fire, apart from the stone churches and a couple of stone built houses, one of which is the Welsh House (of 1595) in Market Square, its name a reminder of the days when Welsh cattle drovers would bring their cattle to Northampton Market, and the other is the 17th-century Hazelrigg House in Mare Fair. After the fire of 1675 the town was rebuilt around what is one of the largest market squares in England, resulting in what the writer Daniel Defoe (1661-1731) described as 'the handsomest and best built town in all this part of England'.

NORTHAMPTON, MARKET PLACE & MOBBS MEMORIAL
1922 72168

It is not surprising, given its long and dramatic history, that there are a number of ghost stories associated with Northampton, and several of its pubs are linked with mysterious activity. Perhaps a spectral memory of the Great Fire of Northampton of 1675 is the explanation for the unnerving sound of crying children and the smell of smoke and burning timber that was reported by a former landlord and his wife at the Auctioneers pub in Market Square in the late 20th century – all the buildings in the Market Square area were destroyed during the fire.

Another haunted pub in Northampton's town centre is the King William IV in Commercial Street. Known to locals as the King Billy, the pub was investigated in recent years by the Northants Haunted group, which concluded that the building was inhabited by no less than six ghosts, one of which had the initials 'J G'. One of the spirits in the building is said to be that of an elderly woman who roams an upper corridor, but she appears to be friendly – when some of the Northants Haunted group held their séance in the corridor, the word 'Welcome' was spelled out to them. According to the group, the ghostly lady is the spirit of a woman who died in 1728 aged 58, who spelled out her name as 'Jakqhalelcm', and said that she haunted the building because she was searching for a loved one she had lost. Further investigations in the main part of the old bar revealed the spirit presence of a man who died in 1914, perhaps during the First World War, and also that of a man called George, who died in 1949 but returns to his local in spirit form. The cellar of the pub is also believed to be subject to much paranormal activity, which may be the cause of the fire alarm in the pub being regularly activated for no obvious reason.

NORTHAMPTON, ST GILES STREET c1955
N40015

Unexplained footsteps have been heard in the Old Black Lion on Black Lion Hill in Northampton, where beer barrels are sometimes moved around by unseen hands, lights are mysteriously turned on and off, and there have been reported sightings of ghostly customers in the building, including an indistinct form of a man with a dog in one room, and a spectral lady on the stairs. The sound of voices in empty corridors of the building has also been reported.

The Wig and Pen in St Giles Street (also formerly known as the Black Lion) is said to have a spooky entity in its basement, of which dogs are particularly scared. There have also been many reports of the sound of a crying baby coming through the back wall of the pub; in 1892 this wall was shared with an adjoining butcher's warehouse, in which Andrew MacRae murdered his mistress Annie Pritchard and their young baby. Annie's dismembered body was found in a sack by the roadside on the way to East Haddon, and MacRae was arrested and hanged for her murder, but the body of her baby was never found – perhaps its spirit is crying, hoping its early body will be found and laid to rest…

NORTHAMPTON, THE DRAPERY 1949 N40005

The Shipman's pub in The Drapery in Northampton is said to be haunted by the ghost of a former manager, Harry Franklin, who killed himself in the building about one hundred years ago in gruesome circumstances – according to a newspaper report of the time, Harry Franklin slit his own throat in the pub, but it took a week for him to die. His unhappy shade is believed to be responsible for poltergeist activity in the pub, including full pint glasses moving around on the bar tables until they drop off, apparently pushed by an unseen hand, strange bumping noises in the night, and the unexplained sounds of footsteps on the stairs and in the bathroom in the depths of the night. A mysterious 'ghostly figure' also appeared in a photograph taken in the pub, standing by the fruit machine.

Like many theatres in the country, the Royal Theatre in Guildhall Road in Northampton has its resident ghost, a 'Grey Lady', who has been seen sitting in one of the boxes overlooking the stage, appears backstage, moves props around and sometimes causes the electric system to play up.

There were various monasteries and friaries in medieval Northampton. These included a wealthy Cluniac monastery, St Andrew's Priory, founded around 1100. Although it is long gone, it is commemorated in the names of St Andrew's Street and Priory Street. There was also a house of Augustinian canons, St James's Abbey, which stood west of the river and is commemorated in the St James area of Northampton. There were three friaries: a Franciscan (Grey Friars) friary founded in 1226 which is now remembered in the name of Greyfriars Street near the bus station; a Blackfriars (Dominican) friary, founded around 1230 and sited near Horse Market; and a Whitefriars (Carmelite) friary, founded in 1271. The Grosvenor Shopping Centre in Union Street in Northampton is believed to have been built on the site of the old Franciscan friary, and is reputed to be haunted by a ghostly friar. There were reports of a mysterious hooded figure in the area in Victorian times, and many people have described feeling uneasy, overcome by the sensation that they were not alone, whilst they were in the delivery corridors on the north of the site. Apparent sightings of the spectral figure of the ghostly friar have also been reported by cleaners working at the centre after the shops have closed, and other people have claimed to have spotted the phantom around the Abington Street entrance of the Grosvenor Centre.

NORTHAMPTON, ABINGTON STREET AND NOTRE DAME HIGH SCHOOL 1922 72172

Towards the end of the 20th century the old town centre of Northampton was subject to much redevelopment. One of Northampton's now-lost haunted buildings is seen in the photograph above of Abington Street in 1922, where a tramcar is passing the forbidding brickwork of the old Notre Dame High School. This was built in 1871 as a school and convent run by the Sisters of Notre Dame de Namur. A former teacher at the school was believed to haunt the building. The ghost was only seen from the knees up, and it is believed that the floor level of the hall that she walks across had been raised since the teacher's death. The school has now been demolished and replaced with shops and offices. Another of Northampton's lost haunted buildings was a house at 18 Horsemarket, now demolished, which was said to be haunted over a long period by a ghostly lady wearing a black lace dress and white gloves.

At Christmas time the moaning shade of an unsavoury character called 'Captain Slash', (real name George Catherall) is said to roam the ruined church of St John the Baptist beside the village green at Boughton, near Northampton. He was the leader of a gang that terrorised the district in the early 1800s, whose crimes included demanding protection money from stallholders at the important horse fair that used to be held on Boughton Green. Captain Slash was eventually captured and hanged at Northampton in 1826. His mother had foreseen that he would come to a bad end and warned him that he would die with his boots on, meaning that he would not have a peaceful death in his bed, but he managed to prove her prediction wrong by kicking off his boots just before his hanging.

South of Northampton is Delapré Abbey, the former Convent of St Mary De La Pré, founded around 1145 as a Cluniac nunnery. The 'second battle of Northampton' was fought on the northern edge of Delapré Abbey's grounds on 10th July 1460 (the 'first battle of Northampton' took place at the site of Northampton Castle in 1264, when the forces of Henry III overran the supporters of Simon de Montfort). It was a crucial battle of the Wars of the Roses, between the Yorkists and the Lancastrians. The Yorkists were victorious and captured the Lancastrian King Henry VI, who was kept prisoner for the night at Delapré Abbey. After the battle the nuns from the abbey tended to the wounded, and many of the soldiers who were killed in the combat were buried in the nuns' graveyard, now the walled garden in the grounds of the abbey. Delapré Abbey was dissolved by Henry VIII in 1538, the estate was sold into private ownership, and the abbey buildings were converted into a handsome country house set in beautiful formal gardens. Although much of the present Grade II listed building was constructed in the second half of the 18th century, Delapré Abbey is reputedly haunted by a mysterious 'Blue Lady' who has been seen many times on the main staircase of the house; it is assumed that she is the shade of a former nun at the abbey, as the Cluniac nuns wore blue habits.

ALTHORP PARK, THE HOUSE 1922 72211

North-west of Northampton is Althorp House, which dates back to the 16th century (photograph 72211, above). At that time John Spencer, a Warwickshire sheep farmer, acquired the estate and created a park of some 300 acres there. Building work began in 1573, in the reign of Queen Elizabeth I, and the great house has been in the ownership of the Spencer family ever since. Althorp was the childhood home of Lady Diana Spencer, who married Charles, Prince of Wales in 1984; as Diana, Princess of Wales, she was laid to rest on an island in the grounds of the Althorp estate after her tragic and untimely death in 1997. The safety of Althorp House is said to be guarded by the careful ghost of an old servant from the past, who checks bedrooms at night where a light has been left on to make sure that no one has fallen asleep and left a lighted candle burning.

Brockhall Hall in the village of Brockhall, west of Northampton, was built between 1580 and 1620 by Edward Eyton. The mansion was later sold to Thomas Thornton, who supported the Parliamentary cause during the Civil War of the 17th century but was pardoned by King Charles II after he was restored to the throne in 1660. The hall has had an eventful history, including being used during the Second World War as the centre of operations for the American Office of Strategic Studies, a predecessor of the CIA, but it has now been converted into private residential apartments. The hall is said to be haunted by a ghostly 'White Lady' who some people think is the unquiet shade of the wife of a former owner of the hall, who committed suicide in the 1780s. The restless spirit does not seem to bother the residents of the hall as she roams around – a member of the residents' committee told the Daily Telegraph newspaper in November 2005 that the entity is 'a very amiable and happy presence that has never caused the committee any concern'.

East of Northampton is the village of Castle Ashby. The historic Falcon Hotel (built in the 1590s) in the village was formerly a blacksmith's forge and is said to be haunted by the ghost of 'Arthur', a blacksmith who worked there during the time of the Civil War of the 17th century. The story goes that he refused the request of some Parliamentarian soldiers to shoe their horses, and they hanged him from a walnut tree in the garden for his stubborn loyalty to the Royalist cause. There is still a walnut tree in the hotel's garden, but it is not known whether it is the same tree where the unfortunate Arthur met his death. Arthur's ghost is believed to visit the bar in the hotel from time to time, and to be the reason that bottles have been seen mysteriously moving about, apparently shifted by an unseen hand – is he helping himself to a little drink?

The 40ft-high stone obelisk shown in the photograph on the opposite page can be found a short distance north of the attractive village of Naseby, west of Rothwell. It was erected in 1823 by the local lord of the manor to commemorate the Civil War battle of Naseby, which was fought on 14th June 1645, just north of the A14. In this battle, Parliament's New Model Army (with Sir Thomas Fairfax as Commander-in-Chief and Oliver Cromwell as Lieutenant-General of the Horse) decisively defeated a Royalist force under King Charles I. The battle was one of the most important engagements of the Civil War, the point at which the tide of war turned against Charles I and in favour of Parliament, ultimately securing the future of Parliamentary democracy and leading to Charles I's eventual defeat and execution. For many years after the battle it was said that spectres re-enacted the conflict in the skies over the battlefield on its anniversary each year, with the sounds of cannons firing and the shrieks of dying men being heard, and local people used to gather on hillsides near the site to watch the spectacle. There were also tales of a phantom procession of men pushing carts along a nearby lane at the time of the anniversary of the battle. In 2008 the Northamptonshire Chronicle published a photograph that was taken by a member of the Northampton Paranormal Group at the battlefield site on the anniversary of the battle of Naseby which appeared to show a ghostly Royalist soldier, although no one was there when the photograph was taken.

**NASEBY
THE MONUMENT
c1955** N200001

DAVENTRY, THE BURTON MEMORIAL AND MOOT HALL c1950 D83003

Daventry was a small market town until the closing decades of the 20th century, when it expanded enormously. In the ninth century Daventry was in the Danelaw, the area of England under Danish rule and law. The town's name, recorded as 'Daventre' in the Middle Ages, is thought to mean 'Daffa's tree'. This might have been misread from a medieval document as 'Danetre' and related to a tree on Borough Hill, the Dane Tree, where the Danes' moot, or court, was held. In the 18th century Daventry grew prosperous on the coaching trade – at its peak, up to 80 stagecoaches a day passed through the town. Dominating this photograph of Daventry's Market Square are the Burton Memorial, erected in 1907 in memory of Edmund Charles Burton – 'a staunch churchman, a renowned sportsman and a man greatly beloved' – and the tall Moot Hall on the right. The Moot Hall was originally a fine Georgian town house which became the residence of the Town Council around 1800, a role which continued until the 1970s. Over the years the Moot Hall has also been used for a variety of other purposes, including a women's prison, the mayor's parlour, a museum and tourist information centre and a restaurant.

Photograph D83021 (below) shows the Wheatsheaf Hotel on Sheaf Street in Daventry as it looked around 1950. The Wheatsheaf is one of Daventry's oldest inns and is linked with one of Northamptonshire's most famous ghost stories. According to local legend, King Charles I stayed at the Wheatsheaf Inn shortly before the Civil War battle of Naseby in 1645, and was visited there on two consecutive nights by the ghost of his friend and counsellor Thomas Wentworth, 1st Earl of Strafford, whose execution had been demanded by Parliament in 1641; the phantom pleaded with the king not to engage the Parliamentarian army, but to continue his march northwards. The shaken king paid great heed to the warning and was minded to take the phantom's advice, but finally followed the advice of his generals and his nephew Prince Rupert to go ahead and engage the enemy, resulting in the disastrous defeat of his Royalist forces. Not surprisingly, Charles I was later heard to remark that he wished he had taken the supernatural advice he had been given in the Daventry inn.

DAVENTRY, THE WHEATSHEAF HOTEL c1950 D83021

According to local folklore, the ghost of a woman riding a spectral white horse haunts Badby Woods, south of Daventry. It is believed to be the shade of an unfaithful wife who was killed by her husband after he found out about her adultery. He waylaid her in the woods and murdered her as she was either on her way to meet her lover or returning from her tryst. Nearby is the historic Fawsley Hall, now a hotel and restaurant; the hall itself is said to be haunted by a ghostly 'White Lady', but its grounds are roamed by a more sinister entity, a spectral huntsman dressed in green who reputedly appears on New Year's Eve, riding a grey horse. No one knows who he is or why he appears, but you would not want to see him – a sighting of his phantom is a warning that your death, or the death of someone close to you, is imminent. The ghostly huntsman seems to be particularly linked with the now-ruined Dower House in Fawsley Park.

THE GUNPOWDER PLOTTERS

Each year on Bonfire Night, November 5th, bonfires are lit and fireworks are let off all over Britain to celebrate the failure of the Gunpowder Plot of 5th November 1605. This was an attempt by a band of conspirators to blow up the House of Lords during the state opening of Parliament, which it was hoped would result in the death of King James I, his young heir, and many other lords. The plotters were devout Roman Catholics who had trusted James 1 to allow them freedom of worship. When he reneged on his promise they planned to blow up the Houses of Parliament whilst King James was in it, together with all his lords and bishops. The plot was foiled when one of the conspirators, Guy Fawkes, was discovered in the cellars beneath the House of Lords ready to set fire to the fuse which would explode the many barrels of gunpowder that had been stored there in readiness for the atrocity. Guy Fawkes was questioned under torture and revealed the identities of the other conspirators; they were hunted down and some were killed whilst resisting arrest, including the plotters' leader, Robert Catesby, or were captured, tried and executed, including Guy Fawkes. The ghost of Guy Fawkes is said to haunt the manor house in the Northamptonshire village of Ashby St Ledgers, north of Daventry, which was the family home of Robert Catesby, and where Guy Fawkes stayed for some weeks prior to the assassination attempt. The half-timbered gatehouse of the manor, next to the village church, is where the Gunpowder Plotters met to hatch their plans, and is known as the 'Plotters Room'.

Photograph B283391, opposite, captures a charming rural scene at Blisworth, south of Northampton. In the foreground is the Grand Union Canal (formerly known as the Grand Junction Canal), with the houses of Blisworth and the 15th-century tower of the village's parish church to be seen on the opposite bank. During the 18th century, Blisworth was the venue for loading and unloading boats from London, the Midlands and the North. Between Blisworth and Stoke Bruerne the Grand Union Canal runs through the famous two-mile long Blisworth Tunnel, one of the longest canal tunnels in Britain and a major feat of engineering. Construction on the tunnel, which is wide enough for two narrowboats to pass each other, began in 1793. However, in the early years of construction there was a tragic accident when the navvies hit quicksand and the tunnel collapsed, killing 14 workmen. A new alignment was found for the construction of the tunnel and it finally opened for through traffic in 1805. A further tragedy occurred in 1861, when two people died in the tunnel due to poor ventilation after a collision between a narrow boat and a steamboat, which filled the tunnel with smoke; two crewmen who were 'legging' the narrowboat through the tunnel were overcome by the smoke fumes – one died from asphyxiation, whilst the other fell unconscious into the canal and drowned. Nowadays the canal is mainly used for recreational purposes, but many people travelling through the canal on leisure craft have felt an echo of these sad events from the past, and the Blisworth Tunnel is widely believed to be haunted. There have been reports of the unexplained sounds of coughing and choking, and of a splash, as if someone has fallen into the water, and what appears to be flickering candlelight has been seen at the spot where the original collapsed tunnel would have intersected with the current tunnel – perhaps ghostly navvies are still working there, even now...

The Admiral Nelson Inn in Dark Lane at Braunston, north-west of Daventry, is situated halfway up the Braunston Lock flight that carries the Grand Union Canal up to the Braunston Tunnel. The inn is supposed to be haunted by a mysterious, shadowy man dressed in old fashioned black clothing who has been seen apparently passing through a bricked up doorway into the adjacent building, Nelson Cottage – presumably this was the way into the hostelry that he was accustomed to using in the past when he popped into the inn for a drop of liquid refreshment.

BLISWORTH, THE GRAND UNION CANAL c1955 B283391

In the extreme south of Northamptonshire is Passenham, near Milton Keynes. Several ghost stories are linked with the village, but the most famous haunted location in Passenham is the picturesque old watermill. Many years ago a young woman from nearby Deanshanger, Nancy Webb, threw herself into the millrace in despair following the death of her husband in the Crimean War (1853-1856) and then the loss of her new-born son. Her ghostly white figure, carrying her child in her arms, is said to glide towards the mill race on the night of the Deanshanger Feast (celebrated in October each year) to re-enact her suicide, and it said that the sound of her screaming can be heard around the millpond at night. Another well-known local ghost of Passenham is that of Sir Robert Bannister (or Banastre), an unpopular local landlord in the 17th century, who lived at the manor house in the village. He fell from his horse and broke his neck whilst out hunting, but one of his feet was caught in a stirrup and he was dragged home by his horse, his body bouncing along the road as his steed made its way back to the manor house in the village. It is said that on dark and stormy nights a phantom steed dragging its gruesome burden can be seen making its way back to the manor house and then moving away towards the village churchyard. His ghost, known as 'wicked Bobby Banister' is also said to drive a spectral horse-drawn carriage around the village.

Another village on the extreme southern border of Northamptonshire is Middleton Cheney. Carpenters Lane in the village is said to be haunted by the shade of 'Nan Gan', who appears on Halloween night. Local folklore said that she was a witch, but in fact she was an old shepherdess who lived alone in a hut in a corner of a nearby field. Another haunted location in the village is the Dolphin Inn, where a mysterious lady dressed in an old-fashioned dark blue, or black, gown has been seen by several people. Her shade does not come into the building in the usual way but via the old front door, now located behind the bar; not everyone can see her, but her visitations are accompanied by a sudden drop in temperature. According to local legend she is the phantom of a regular customer in the past who was partial to a glass of Guinness, known as 'Old Mrs Waters'. In her earthly life she liked to sit in a favourite spot beside a window in the pub; there have been a number of sightings of her ghost sitting there, and also in the passageway along the side of the main pub building.

In south Northamptonshire is the former hunting ground of Whittlewood Forest. The Forest mainly covers an area between Silverstone, Syresham and Abthorpe, but also includes Bucknell Wood, Whistley Wood and other woodland areas around the village of Whittlebury, which are said to be haunted by a ghostly hunting party. On wild nights you may hear the sound of baying hounds and galloping horses on the wind, as a ghostly knight and his pack of hounds pursue their prey – the spirit of the beautiful daughter of a forestry official from medieval times. The knight fell hopelessly in love with the maiden, but she cruelly teased and tormented him. Her rejection drove the knight mad, and in his anguish he killed himself with his own sword; the sin of his suicide condemned his spirit to roam for ever, never able to rest. The maiden herself died soon afterwards, and the phantom knight eternally pursues her shade through the forest with his hellhounds, trying to hunt her down and punish her for the capricious behaviour that damned his soul.

The picturesque village of Ecton is between Northampton and Wellingborough. On the edge of the village is the World's End pub, which tradition says was used as a temporary prison for Royalist soldiers captured at the Civil War battle of Naseby in 1645. Many soldiers died there from their wounds, and in later years the cellar of the pub is said to have been used as a mortuary, so it is not surprising that the building has gained a reputation for its busy ghostly activity over the years. The sound of disembodied footsteps in the cellar has been reported by several landlords, and mysterious shadowy figures have also been glimpsed there. On one occasion in recent years, a spectral man was seen there by a workman who described the apparition as only being visible from the knees up – presumably the phantom was walking on an earlier, lower, floor lever. The ghost of a former barmaid at the pub, known as 'Angel', is also said to haunt the building. The local tale is that she was killed by her lover in a fit of jealous rage, and his shade also roams the building, but the two spirits never meet. The village of Ecton is also said to be haunted by a phantom nun, whose face appears as a fleshless skull. Local lore says that she appears at midnight every Halloween beside the road outside the village where the local gibbet used to stand, where felons were hanged and their bodies were left to hang as an example to others. If anyone attempts to pass by on the road, the spectre attempts to stop them. The phantom nun is also said to have appeared at the World's End pub.

WELLINGBOROUGH, SILVER STREET c1950 W279005

WELLINGBOROUGH, THE HIND HOTEL c1950 W279009

Wellingborough, an ancient market town, grew up at the crossroads of two major routes. Wellingborough developed rapidly in the second half of the 20th century, when it became a London overspill town, and the growth of the town has entailed much redevelopment, but the past is still very much present in the town's plan and architecture. The Hind Hotel in Sheep Street (seen in photograph W279009, above) is one of Wellingborough's best surviving older buildings and a former coaching inn. It dates from the 1640s and is built in the local russet ironstone with limestone dressings; its central carriageway was blocked and the timber porch built around 1900. Oliver Cromwell is said to have stayed at the Hind in 1645, en route to the Civil War battle of Naseby in June 1645, and his shade may still visit the hotel – in 2002 a medium claimed to have spoken to his spirit there. Another spirit said to haunt the hotel is that of a small child, which has been heard crying in the building late at night, even when no children are in residence....

Another building in Wellingborough that is reputed to be haunted is Rafferty's pub in Market Street, said to be roamed by a ghostly man dressed in old-fashioned clothing of a long black jacket and white knee-length socks; he has been described as looking like a Quaker, similar to the man on the Quaker Oats packet. He is said to particularly frequent the alley behind the pub, but has also been seen inside the building by several customers. He also manifests his presence with mild poltergeist activity, such as slamming doors and moving objects about.

The village of Walgrave, north west of Wellingborough, is said to have a resident ghost in the shape of a female spirit that roams the area wearing a wedding gown. Local legend claims that she is the ghost of a young woman who was murdered on her wedding night, and was buried in her bridal dress.

WELLINGBOROUGH, MARKET STREET c1955 W279029

The historic coaching inn of the Green Dragon Hotel at Higham Ferrers near Rushden is rumoured to have a resident ghost in Room 3. Over the years the hotel has been subject to various bouts of paranormal activity, including the sound of mysterious voices, unexplained knocking and banging sounds, and glasses seemingly pushed along the bar until they fall off the edge. The hotel was visited in January 2009 by East Midlands Paranormal Investigators who investigated various areas around the building; they reported hearing strange knocking, banging and whistling sounds, and detected mysterious movement around the bar area as well as a strange white light in other parts of the building. However, all the paranormal activity seems to be of a playful nature, and is in no way of malicious intent. Another haunted pub in Higham Ferrers is the Griffin in the High Street, where mysterious footsteps have been heard when no one is there, and lights are turned on and off by an unseen hand. A former landlord of the Griffin reported that he and his wife were sometimes woken up by the sound of loud music coming from a tape player which had been switched off when the pub had closed for the night…

According to local legend, the unhappy ghost of poor Lydia Atley (sometimes known as Astley, or Atlee) roams around the village of Ringstead, a few miles north of Raunds. A 'weak minded' girl of dubious reputation, she had been seduced by the village butcher, William Weekly Ball, a married man, and was in the final stages of pregnancy with his child when she disappeared without trace in July 1850 after the couple had been overheard by several people quarrelling violently in Ball's orchard. A few days later one of the villagers received a letter from a son in Northampton saying that Lydia had been seen in the town with a male companion, but it later turned out that William Weekly Ball had asked the writer to send the letter. The local police investigated Lydia's disappearance and offered a reward for information, but could find no clues to her whereabouts or fate, and the following year, William Weekly Ball moved away from the village. In February 1864, thirteen years after she vanished, the skeleton of a woman was found in a ditch, which was assumed to be Lydia's remains, although this could not be proved – there was no sign of the baby, although the doctor who gave evidence at the trial said "Supposing the woman had been in the family way, as stated, I believe all foetal bones would have been obliterated from long interment". Although it was possible that Lydia's baby had been born just before her disappearance, the doctor could see no sign of the woman whose remains were found ever having given birth, and it was known that Lydia had already had one illegitimate child, so he concluded that the skeleton was probably not hers; also, the skeleton was found in an area that was traditionally said to have been used by Gypsies as a burial place for their dead. However, another village man gave evidence that he had drawn one of Lydia's teeth for her a few weeks before her disappearance, and the skeleton did indeed have a missing tooth to match his evidence. William Weekly Ball was arrested and charged with Lydia's murder but was acquitted for lack of proof, and Lydia's true fate and the whereabouts of her remains is still a mystery. However, local people were sure that Ball was guilty of her murder, and a song was soon circulating in the district with the chorus:

'O cruel butcher he hung should be,
For killing of Lydia Atley.'

Perhaps this miscarriage of justice is why Lydia's ghost is said to haunt the village. According to local tradition, her spectre appears at midnight, walking from the orchard where she was probably murdered towards the churchyard, and then moves east – perhaps towards the place where her remains still lie undiscovered, so that she can be buried in sanctified ground.

Near Ringstead is Woodford, which has a strange and gruesome relic in its parish church of St Mary – a human heart, wrapped in cloth, which is set into a glass-fronted cavity in one of the pillars of the north aisle of the church. There is a long-held story that during the religious turmoil of the mid 16th century the vicar of St Mary's Church, John Styles, lost his living because of his Catholic beliefs and fled abroad to live in a monastery in Belgium, taking with him a valuable chalice from the church. Some years later his successor to the Woodford parish, Andrew Powlet, went to Belgium to retrieve the chalice; he found that John Styles had since died, so Powlet returned to Woodford with the chalice and as a kindness he also brought back John's heart to rest in his former parish that he had been forced to leave. Andrew Powlet secretly placed the heart in a cavity of the pillar of the church, and placed the chalice for safekeeping in a secret cavity in the rectory, where it remained hidden for centuries. In 1862 the young vicar who then had the living of Woodford was visited in what was then the rectory (now known as Glebe Hall Farm) by the apparition of Andrew Powlett, which appeared to him hovering in the hallway and pointing to the secret cavity, which was subsequently discovered and found to contain the chalice and a letter which led to the discovery of John Styles's heart in the pillar. However, in the 1990s a time capsule left by Reverend Smythe, who was rector of the church during its restorations in the 1860s, described how the heart was found by workmen during the restoration work. It is not known whose heart it is, or why it was placed in the cavity of the pillar, but the most likely theory is that is was the heart of a former lord of the manor who died whilst on pilgrimage to the Holy Land in the Middle Ages and whose heart was brought home – although it is a mystery as to why it was placed in the pillar. The church is also famous for other ghostly activity – in 1964 two schoolboys visited the church and took some photographs; when they were developed, one of them showed a mysterious green, transparent figure kneeling by the altar, although the boys were alone in the church at the time. Their camera and the film were examined by experts, but nothing untoward or evidence of tampering with the image was found, and the explanation for the image remains a mystery. A further ghostly sighting was reported in the early years of the 21st century, when a woman reported seeing a strange white shape coming towards her in the same area of the church. Is this apparition linked with the mysterious heart in the pillar, or is it perhaps the shade of a former rector, still kneeling at the altar in prayer? Who knows…

Clopton, south of Oundle, is famous for the ghostly activity of the delightfully-named 'Skulking Dudley', an unsavoury character from the Middle Ages who lived at Clopton Manor. He was a cruel and unpopular lord of the manor, renowned in his lifetime for bullying his tenants and workforce, and eventually he was killed with a scythe by one of his harvesters whilst he was whipping him, after his abuse became too much to bear. His spirit continued to torment the local people after his death, and it is said that for many centuries the ghost of Skulking Dudley roamed the area at night, frightening the descendants of those villagers who had crossed him in his earthly life. Eventually the local people got so fed up with the malignant spirit that in the early 20th century they arranged to get the spirit exorcised – Dudley's malevolent force was so strong that it took no less than 12 clergymen to lay his ghost to rest. This unpleasant character from the area's past is recalled in the name of Skulking Dudley Copse near the village.

OUNDLE, NEW STREET c1950 O103029

A few miles north of Oundle, in the north east corner of Northamptonshire, is the site of the former Fotheringhay (or Fotheringay) Castle, where the ill-fated Mary, Queen of Scots was held prisoner in her final days and where she met her death. The fugitive Scottish queen had been kept in 'honourable custody' in England by her cousin Queen Elizabeth I for nearly 20 years, transferred from castle to castle whilst Elizabeth decided what to do with her. Eventually it was discovered that Mary had became involved in a plot to assassinate Elizabeth and take her throne, and she was put on trial for treason. In October 1586 Mary was tried in Fotheringay Castle, and found guilty; in February 1587 she was executed by beheading in the Great Hall of the castle. The castle later fell into disrepair, and its remains were demolished in the 17th century. There is now nothing left of Fotheringhay Castle to see except for the mound on which it stood, but there is a vestige of the former grandeur of its interior in the Talbot Hotel in the centre of Oundle, seen on the left of photograph O103029 on the previous pages. The striking façade of the Talbot Hotel was largely rebuilt in 1625, using stone from Fotheringhay Castle. The inn's splendid oak staircase also came from the castle, bought by the Talbot Hotel's former landlord William Whitwell. It was down this staircase that Mary, Queen of Scots came on her way to her execution, and it is said that her ghost still descends this way. What sounds like the disembodied footsteps of a woman has been heard on it, and it is said that the ghost of a woman wearing a long white gown has been seen at the top of the staircase. The queen's spectre is also said to sometimes look out of the hotel from a window on the landing, although she can only be seen by men – she can be recognised by the white cap she wears. The mysterious sound of a woman crying bitterly at night was also once reported by a guest in the hotel, coming from a room that was empty – it was later realised that the date was the anniversary of Queen Mary's execution…

The Talbot Hotel is not the only haunted inn in Oundle. Another haunted hostelry in the town is the Ship Inn in West Street. Local legend says that the building is haunted by the restless spirit of a former landlord who killed himself many years ago by throwing himself to his death out of a bedroom window. Customers in the pub and several landlords over the years have claimed to have seen his ghost, and people have reported feeling something invisible brush past them on the stairs...

OUNDLE, WEST STREET c1950 O103028

South-east of Oundle is Barnwell, which was formerly two separate villages with their own parish churches, Barnwell All Saints and Barnwell St Andrew. Both medieval churches are still in use, although only the chancel remains of All Saints' Church, the rest having been demolished in 1825. Near the entrance to the graveyard of All Saints' Church is an ancient tombstone carved with an image of a monk-like figure, which may have given rise to the story that a phantom monk haunts the All Saints area of Barnwell. Is this the same spectral monk that is said to haunt the impressive ruins of the 13th-century Barnwell Castle within the gardens of the manor house north of the village? The ghost is said to be faceless beneath the hood of his habit, and brandishes a whip which he cracks from time to time and which is supposed to be the cause of sudden gusts of wind that have been felt in the castle area even on windless days. According to local legend, the phantom is the restless shade of a monk who was murdered in medieval times. Barnwell Castle is private property and is not open to the public, but it is visible from the road.

North of Oundle is Apethorpe Hall, a Grade I listed country house (part of which dates back to the 15th century) that has recently been the subject of a major restoration programme under the auspices of English Heritage. Apethorpe Hall's state apartment suite was rebuilt in 1622-1624 to receive King James I, and the mansion still contains one of the finest sets of Jacobean interiors of the period, with decorative plaster ceilings, fireplaces and panelling.

In earlier times, Apethorpe Hall was owned by Sir Walter Mildmay (1523-1589), who was Chancellor of the Exchequer to Queen Elizabeth I, and Apethorpe was one of the queen's favourite places to stop when she was travelling in the area. Apethorpe Hall passed from Sir Walter Mildmay to his son Sir Anthony Mildmay (1547-1617) and his wife, Grace. Lady Grace Mildmay was famous for making and dispensing home-brewed medicines for her neighbours and was particularly famous for her charity and generosity. She would often distribute money to the children of the area, and after her death in 1620 her ghost was said to haunt the corridors of Apethorpe Hall, where her spirit reputedly glided around the building scattering ethereal coins... According to the tale, Lady Grace's spirit used to emerge from a portrait of her which hung in the long gallery, but unfortunately this was lost in a fire at the Hall many years ago. The last sighting of her ghost was several decades ago when Apethorpe Hall was being used as a school, when it was seen floating down a staircase. However, it is said that if you do see Lady Grace's phantom and approach her, she will give you some money.

In Norman and medieval times, Rockingham Forest in the north-east of Northamptonshire was one of the many areas of the country which had been designated a royal hunting ground by William I and his successors. The picturesque village of Rockingham stands on a steep hill above the River Welland in the heart of the great Rockingham Forest; from the summit you can look out over five counties. Rockingham used to be a market town for the surrounding area but the market ceased years ago, although the old market cross still stands in the village. Above the village of Rockingham lies a splendid castle. The earliest castle there was a motte and bailey structure built by order of William the Conqueror, and the first stone castle on the site was founded by his son, William II ('William Rufus'). For 500 years Rockingham Castle was used as a royal residence and hunting lodge. Although relatively little of the medieval castle remains, the late 13th-century gatehouse survives, with the arched gateway flanked by massive drum towers.

ROCKINGHAM, THE CASTLE c1960 R353009

ROCKINGHAM, THE CASTLE c1960 R353319

Described as ruinous in the early 16th century, Rockingham Castle's character beyond the mighty walls is now that of a Tudor and 17th-century country house. In the 19th century the owners of the castle were the Watsons, who were great friends with the author Charles Dickens. Dickens stayed at Rockingham Castle, and wrote part of his novel 'Bleak House' there, using the castle as the inspiration for Chesney Wold in the book, the home of the characters Sir Leicester Dedlock and Lady Honoria Dedlock. Whilst staying at Rockingham Castle, Charles Dickens claimed to have seen a ghostly figure that moved through the grounds towards an iron gate and then disappeared; perhaps the shadowy figure that Dickens saw was a spectre from the time when the castle was taken by Cromwell's forces during the Civil War of the 17th century.

CORBY, CORPORATION STREET c1965 C337060

Smarts
SMARTS
TIMPSON SHOES

It is difficult to imagine that the modern thriving industrial town of Corby was once an obscure Rockingham Forest village, with a population of around 200 people, but it was, and a fine one at that, with the right to hold a weekly market and two annual fairs from the time of King Henry III, and a royal charter dating back to the reign of Queen Elizabeth I, which exempted the men of the village from paying road and bridge tolls throughout the kingdom. One of the fairs, the unique Pole Fair, is still held – only every twenty years though, and the last occasion was in 2001. Much of the modern housing of Corby, especially that in the west around the Kingswood and Danesholme area, is built over Bronze Age, Iron Age and Roman remains, and pottery from the latter era was found in large quantities when building development took place in the open fields and woodland which then surrounded the nascent town. An important Roman road, the so-called Gartree Road, also passed through the southern area of the village, running from Huntingdon to Leicester. The Grade II listed Knights Lodge pub on Tower Hill Road dates from the 17th century and is one of the oldest buildings in Corby. Beneath the pub are the remains of ancient tunnels, accessed from a trapdoor in the floor, which are said to have once linked the building with Rockingham Castle. In medieval times the site of the pub belonged to the Cistercian monks of Pipewell Abbey a few miles south west of the town, and perhaps this link explains the tale that the pub is haunted by a ghostly monk in a hooded robe that glides across the floor of the pub before vanishing into a panelled wall. A former landlady who saw him do this described how her dog also saw the figure, and was so unsettled that it barked and growled at the place where the spectre had disappeared. The monk's shadowy figure has also been spotted lingering around the old inglenook fireplace at one end of the pub. As well as the spectral monk, there seem to be other spirits in residence in the building: the sound of young women chattering and laughing has been heard coming from a bedroom of the inn which was known to be empty, and disembodied footsteps have been heard on the stairs, as well as the sound of whispering. The sound of crying has also been heard in the pub, and is said to emanate from the grieving ghost of a woman whose little daughter died hundreds of years ago after falling down the stairs. However, the regulars think that all this talk of ghosts only adds to the atmosphere of this historic old pub!

GEDDINGTON, VILLAGE 1922 72253

Off the A43 between Kettering and Corby at Geddington village is a minor road to Newton, also known as Newton in the Willows. Take care if you are driving alone along this road, for it is said to be haunted by a mysterious entity that might suddenly appear sitting beside you in your car, and then just as suddenly disappear when you have driven beyond the woods. A similar haunting has been reported at the other end of the minor road, linked with the area known as Barford Bridge, where the old railway bridge crosses the A6003 between Kettering and Corby. In 1984 a police sergeant and a woman driver both reported seeing the face of a bearded, hooded monk in their rear view mirrors, as their ghostly passenger sat in the back seat of their cars. This ghostly phenomenon may be linked with the now-lost hamlet of Barford in the area, where in medieval times a small chapel was served by a monk from Pipewell Abbey, a few miles to the south west.

Pronounced 'Rowell', the town of Rothwell quite possibly takes its name from an old Danish word meaning 'red well'. By the Middle Ages it had become a town of some importance, and a market charter was granted by King John in 1204, as well as permission for an annual fair which is still held here during the week following Trinity Sunday. Rothwell's most famous landmark, the old Market House in the town centre, was built by a local lord of the manor, Thomas Tresham, and designed by William Grumbald. Work began in 1577, but the building remained unfinished until 1895 when J A Gotch, a Northamptonshire architect, roofed it and filled in the arches. It was originally known as Rothwell Cross, and acquired its present name much later. On the central frieze is a Latin inscription dedicating the building to the town and country, and on the upper frieze are 90 coats-of-arms of landed Northamptonshire families. The building is used today as council offices. The historic building has been investigated by Northants Haunted, who reported that they had made contact with a spirit called something like 'Moto', whose earthly life was in the early decades of the 16th century. One member of the group also received a personal message from the spirit that no one else could have known.

ROTHWELL, THE MARKET HOUSE 1922 72249

KETTERING, MARKET 1922 72233

WHOLESALE & EXPORT
VARIETY
CIRCLE
GALLERY

Kettering was once a market town with a small weaving industry. From the 17th century it was a centre for the production of woollen cloth, and later of silk and plush. By the late 19th century the Kettering area had become an important manufacturing centre for boots and shoes, specialising in heavy work boots. The redevelopment of the 20th century has resulted in the demolition of much of the old town centre, but the market place and the Kettering Heritage Quarter are well worth exploring. The building that is currently occupied by a café at 1a Market Street in Kettering is believed to be one of the oldest in the town, and not surprisingly it is linked with a ghost story. The tale goes that in the 18th century a party of soldiers was staying in the Duke's Arms, which stood opposite where the café building is now. With the soldiers was a young drummer boy, who got drunk and became involved in an argument; he was dragged outside to be stabbed to death in a nearby alleyway. The site of that alleyway is now the entrance to the café, and the boy's ghost is said to haunt the building. Several owners of the premises in the 20th century reported feeling uneasy in the premises and noted strange occurrences, including mysterious noises, especially from the stock room, and sudden drops in temperature. At one time the staff refused to go to the stock room alone, even though they had not been told anything about the story of the drummer boy. In the late 20th century, whilst the building was being repaired, a dagger was found in the wall of one of the upstairs rooms, although it is not clear whether this had any link with the death of the drummer boy. The building was investigated in June 2009 by the Northamptonshire Paranormal Investigation Team (when it was the premises of the Tasty Bites restaurant) who saw several sightings of a strange black shadowy form at the top of the stairs and heard someone – or something – giggling at their attempts to locate its presence.

Northamptonshire Paranormal Investigation Team were called in to do another paranormal investigation in Kettering in January 2010, when they investigated the premises of Davis Opticians, at Moyune House in Crispin Place, just off the High Street in the town. The team were invited to investigate the building by the Practice Manager after a number of employees had reported strange experiences that they could not explain, such as the uncanny feeling of being watched by an invisible presence, hearing footsteps in an area of the building where no one was present, and seeing a salt cellar moving across a table in an area of the building where lunch breaks are taken, as if pushed by an unseen hand. The investigators noted a number of sudden drops in temperature in the areas they were investigating which accompanied apparent paranormal activity, such as items being moved, a heavy swivel chair being turned around when it was out of reach of everyone in the room, and a mysterious dark shadow moving away at the bottom of the stairs, which showed up as a series of light orbs when it was filmed. The sound of heavy footsteps was also heard moving along a corridor near the garage entrance, but no one was there. During the night-long investigation several members of the team felt a sensation of something tugging at their clothes, as if trying to attract their attention. The NPIT concluded that a number of ghosts haunt the building, including a small boy in scruffy clothing, a young girl, and an elderly man dressed in a long black coat or cloak and carrying a walking cane, but are malevolent – although the shade of the small boy is a very cheeky character who loves to amuse himself by playing tricks on the staff.

FRANCIS FRITH

PIONEER VICTORIAN PHOTOGRAPHER

Francis Frith, founder of the world-famous photographic archive, was a complex and multi-talented man. A devout Quaker and a highly successful Victorian businessman, he was philosophical by nature and pioneering in outlook. By 1855 he had already established a wholesale grocery business in Liverpool, and sold it for the astonishing sum of £200,000, which is the equivalent today of over £15,000,000. Now in his thirties, and captivated by the new science of photography, Frith set out on a series of pioneering journeys up the Nile and to the Near East.

INTRIGUE AND EXPLORATION

He was the first photographer to venture beyond the sixth cataract of the Nile. Africa was still the mysterious 'Dark Continent', and Stanley and Livingstone's historic meeting was a decade into the future. The conditions for picture taking confound belief. He laboured for hours in his wicker dark-room in the sweltering heat of the desert, while the volatile chemicals fizzed dangerously in their trays. Back in London he exhibited his photographs and was 'rapturously cheered' by members of the Royal Society. His reputation as a photographer was made overnight.

VENTURE OF A LIFE-TIME

By the 1870s the railways had threaded their way across the country, and Bank Holidays and half-day Saturdays had been made obligatory by Act of Parliament. All of a sudden the working man and his family were able to enjoy days out, take holidays, and see a little more of the world.

With typical business acumen, Francis Frith foresaw that these new tourists would enjoy having souvenirs to commemorate their days out. For the next thirty years he travelled the country by train and by pony and trap, producing fine photographs of seaside resorts and beauty spots that were keenly bought by millions of Victorians. These prints were painstakingly pasted into family albums and pored over during the dark nights of winter, rekindling precious memories of summer excursions. Frith's studio was soon supplying retail shops all over the country, and by 1890 F Frith & Co had become the greatest specialist photographic publishing company in the world, with over 2,000 sales outlets, and pioneered the picture postcard.

FRANCIS FRITH'S LEGACY

Francis Frith had died in 1898 at his villa in Cannes, his great project still growing. By 1970 the archive he created contained over a third of a million pictures showing 7,000 British towns and villages.

Frith's legacy to us today is of immense significance and value, for the magnificent archive of evocative photographs he created provides a unique record of change in the cities, towns and villages throughout Britain over a century and more. Frith and his fellow studio photographers revisited locations many times down the years to update their views, compiling for us an enthralling and colourful pageant of British life and character.

We are fortunate that Frith was dedicated to recording the minutiae of everyday life. For it is this sheer wealth of visual data, the painstaking chronicle of changes in dress, transport, street layouts, buildings, housing and landscape that captivates us so much today, offering us a powerful link with the past and with the lives of our ancestors.

Computers have now made it possible for Frith's many thousands of images to be accessed almost instantly. The archive offers every one of us an opportunity to examine the places where we and our families have lived and worked down the years. Its images, depicting our shared past, are now bringing pleasure and enlightenment to millions around the world a century and more after his death.

For further information visit: www.francisfrith.com

INTERIOR DECORATION

Frith's photographs can be seen framed and as giant wall murals in thousands of pubs, restaurants, hotels, banks, retail stores and other public buildings throughout Britain. These provide interesting and attractive décor, generating strong local interest and acting as a powerful reminder of gentler days in our increasingly busy and frenetic world.

FRITH PRODUCTS

All Frith photographs are available as prints and posters in a variety of different sizes and styles. In the UK we also offer a range of other gift and stationery products illustrated with Frith photographs, although many of these are not available for delivery outside the UK – see our web site for more information on the products available for delivery in your country.

THE INTERNET

Over 100,000 photographs of Britain can be viewed and purchased on the Frith web site. The web site also includes memories and reminiscences contributed by our customers, who have personal knowledge of localities and of the people and properties depicted in Frith photographs. If you wish to learn more about a specific town or village you may find these reminiscences fascinating to browse. Why not add your own comments if you think they would be of interest to others? See **www.francisfrith.com**

PLEASE HELP US BRING FRITH'S PHOTOGRAPHS TO LIFE

Our authors do their best to recount the history of the places they write about. They give insights into how particular towns and villages developed, they describe the architecture of streets and buildings, and they discuss the lives of famous people who lived there. But however knowledgeable our authors are, the story they tell is necessarily incomplete.

Frith's photographs are so much more than plain historical documents. They are living proofs of the flow of human life down the generations. They show real people at real moments in history; and each of those people is the son or daughter of someone, the brother or sister, aunt or uncle, grandfather or grandmother of someone else. All of them lived, worked and played in the streets depicted in Frith's photographs.

We would be grateful if you would give us your insights into the places shown in our photographs: the streets and buildings, the shops, businesses and industries. Post your memories of life in those streets on the Frith website: what it was like growing up there, who ran the local shop and what shopping was like years ago; if your workplace is shown tell us about your working day and what the building is used for now. Read other visitors' memories and reconnect with your shared local history and heritage. With your help more and more Frith photographs can be brought to life, and vital memories preserved for posterity, and for the benefit of historians in the future.

Wherever possible, we will try to include some of your comments in future editions of our books. Moreover, if you spot errors in dates, titles or other facts, please let us know, because our archive records are not always completely accurate—they rely on 140 years of human endeavour and hand-compiled records. You can email us using the contact form on the website.

Thank you!

For further information, trade, or author enquiries please contact us at the address below:

The Francis Frith Collection, Oakley Business Park, Wylye Road, Dinton, Wiltshire SP3 5EU.

Tel: +44 (0)1722 716 376 Fax: +44 (0)1722 716 881

e-mail: sales@francisfrith.co.uk **www.francisfrith.com**